JOSEPH MIDTHUN   SAMUEL HITI

BUILDING BLOCKS OF SCIENCE

GRAVITY

WORLD
BOOK

a Scott Fetzer company
Chicago

www.worldbookonline.com

World Book, Inc.
233 N. Michigan Avenue
Chicago, IL 60601
U.S.A.

For information about other World Book publications, visit our website at http://www.worldbookonline.com or call 1-800-WORLDBK (967-5325).

For information about sales to schools and libraries, call 1-800-975-3250 (United States); 1-800-837-5365 (Canada).

Library of Congress Cataloging-in-Publication Data

Gravity.
        p. cm. -- (Building blocks of science)
    Includes index.
    Summary: "A graphic nonfiction volume that introduces the force of gravity and its effects on Earth and the universe. Features include several photographic pages, a glossary, additional resource list, and an index"--Provided by publisher.
    ISBN 978-0-7166-1424-1
    1. Gravity--Juvenile literature. I. World Book, Inc.
QC178.G6826 2011
531'.14--dc23
                                    2011025907

Building Blocks of Science
Set ISBN: 978-0-7166-1420-3

Printed in China by Leo Paper Products LTD., Heshan, Guangdong
1st printing December 2011

Acknowledgments:
Created by Samuel Hiti and Joseph Midthun.
Art by Samuel Hiti. Written by Joseph Midthun.

© Dreamstime 19; © Joel Gordon Photography 9; © Shutterstock 8; WORLD BOOK illustration by Paul Perrault and Brenda Tropinski 18

ATTENTION, READER!

Some characters in this series throw large objects from tall buildings, play with fire, ride on bicycle handlebars, and perform other dangerous acts. However, they are CARTOON CHARACTERS. Please do not try any of these things at home because you could seriously harm yourself—or others around you!

STAFF

Executive Committee
President: Donald D. Keller
Vice President and Editor in Chief: Paul A. Kobasa
Vice President, Marketing/
    Digital Products: Sean Klunder
Vice President, International: Richard Flower
Director, Human Resources: Bev Ecker

Editorial
Associate Manager, Supplementary
    Publications: Cassie Mayer
Writer and Letterer: Joseph Midthun
Editors: Mike DuRoss and Brian Johnson
Researcher: Annie Brodsky
Manager, Contracts & Compliance
    (Rights & Permissions): Loranne K. Shields

Manufacturing/Pre-Press/Graphics and Design
Director: Carma Fazio
Manufacturing Manager: Steven Hueppchen
Production/Technology Manager:
    Anne Fritzinger
Proofreader: Emilie Schrage
Manager, Graphics and Design: Tom Evans
Coordinator, Design Development and
    Production: Brenda B. Tropinski
Book Design: Samuel Hiti
Photographs Editor: Kathy Creech

TABLE OF CONTENTS

What Is Gravity? 4

Measuring Gravity 8

Mass vs. Weight 10

How Objects Fall 12

Friction 14

Inertia 16

Gravity and the Sun 18

Gravity and the Moon 20

Gravity and the Solar System 22

Black Holes................... 26

Why Study Gravity?...................28

Glossary...................30

Find Out More...................31

Index 32

There is a glossary on page 30. Terms defined in the glossary are in type **that looks like this** on their first appearance.

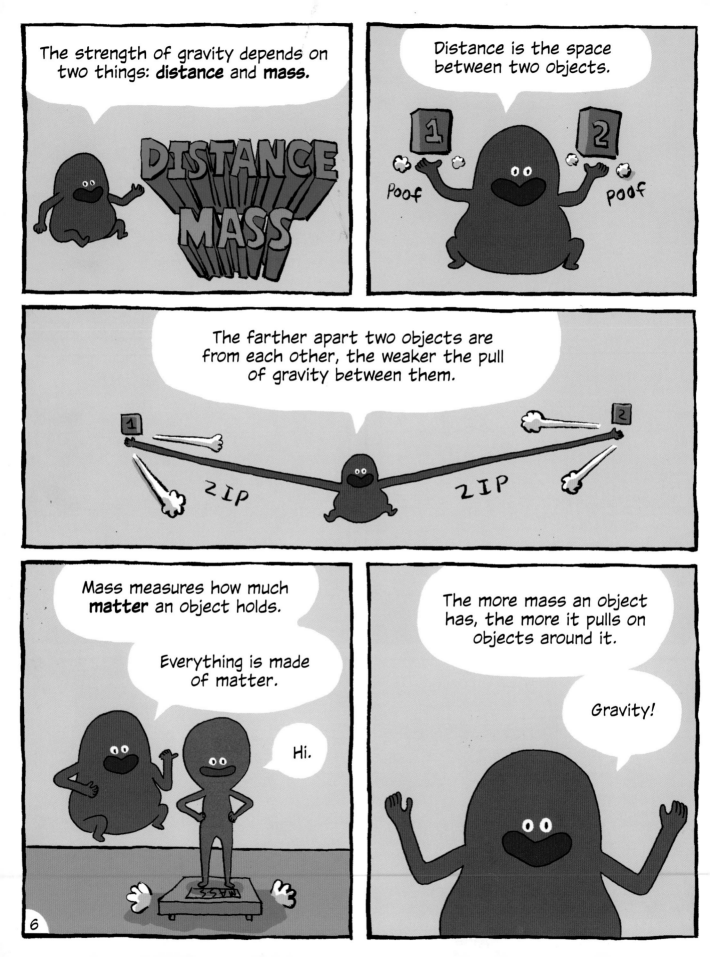

Gravity is an invisible force, but we can still measure it.

Weight is a measure of the pull of gravity on an object.

You've probably weighed things to find out how heavy they are. When we weigh things to find out their mass, we use pounds or kilograms as units of measurement.

TIC
TIC
TIC

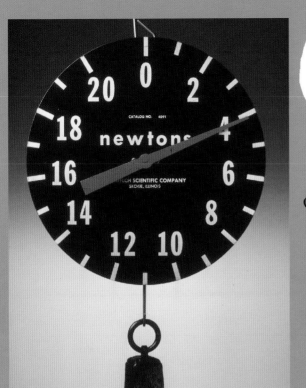

When scientists weigh objects to measure their gravity, they use newtons as units of force.

But remember: whatever unit of measurement you use...

...heavier objects always have a stronger pull of gravity than lighter objects.

13

GRAVITY AND THE SUN

You already know that gravity doesn't just affect things on Earth. The planets, moon, and stars have gravity, too.

The sun's gravity keeps the planets in the **solar system** from hurling off into space.

And inertia is the reason why we don't crash into the sun.

Uranus

Saturn

Venus

Earth

Mercury

SUN

Mars

Neptune

Asteroid belt

Jupiter

Without the sun's gravity, Earth would travel through space in a straight line.

The sun's gravity pulls Earth toward the sun, but Earth is moving very quickly. It spins around and around the sun.

Gravity acts like an invisible string, tethering each planet to the sun.

The motion of the planets prevents them from falling into the sun!

GRAVITY AND THE MOON

Back then, the solar system was a hectic place! Massive clusters of rock and gas moved around the sun, smashing into one another.
Eventually, other particles in the cloud collided and stuck together, forming planets around the sun.
BANG
BOOM
BANG

The moon most likely formed as a result of a giant collision between Earth and another early planet.

As a result of the impact, a cloud of rock shot off Earth's surface and went into orbit.

The cloud cooled and **condensed** into a ring of small, solid planetary bodies.

Gravity brought them together, forming the moon!

BLACK HOLES!
Gravity creates the most violent and powerful objects in the universe...
Black holes form when stars much larger than the sun use up all their fuel.
Stars are massive, so they have tremendous gravity.
Their gravity would cause the stars to collapse if they weren't using fuel to shine.

When a star uses fuel, it releases energy. This energy from inside the star pushes outward.

The star's gravity pulls inward, toward the center of the star.

The star is safe as long as these forces are balanced.

But when the star runs out of fuel, there is nothing to stop the pull of gravity. The star collapses in on itself!

The largest stars keep collapsing until all of their mass collects into one tiny point.

The gravity around a black hole is so powerful it will rip anything apart that comes near.

Nothing can escape the gravity of a black hole—not even light!

GLOSSARY

attract to pull one object toward another.

black hole a region of space whose gravitational force is so strong that nothing can escape it.

condense to make denser or more compact.

distance the amount of space between two points.

force a push or a pull.

friction rubbing between objects that slows them down and produces heat.

gravity a force that attracts all objects toward one another.

inertia the tendency of objects to stay at rest or stay in motion.

mass the amount of matter in an object.

matter what all things are made of.

motion a change in position.

orbit (n.) the path of one object around another determined by gravity. For example, the path of Earth around the sun is an orbit. (v.) to revolve around an object.

solar system the sun and all the planets, satellites, comets, and other heavenly bodies that revolve around it.

speed the distance traveled in a certain time.

universe everything that exists everywhere, including Earth, the stars, planets, and other heavenly bodies.

FIND OUT MORE

Books

Black Holes by Ker Than (Children's Press, 2010)

Cool Gravity Activities: Fun Science Projects About Balance by James Hopwood (ABDO Publishing Company, 2008)

Experiments with Gravity by Salvatore Tocci (Children's Press, 2002)

Gravity by John Farndon (Benchmark Books, 2002)

Isaac Newton and Gravity by Steve Parker (Chelsea House, 1995)

I Fall Down by Vicki Cobb and Julia Gorton (HarperCollins, 2004)

Weight by Chris Woodford (Blackbirch Press, 2005)

What Is Mass? by Don L. Curry (Children's Press, 2004)

Websites

Exploratorium Observatory
http://www.exploratorium.edu/observatory/index.html
At the Exploratorium—part of NASA's Sun-Earth Education Forum—you can learn about gravity and its effects throughout the solar system.

IMSA on Wheels: Force and Inertia
http://www.imsa.edu/programs/kidsinstitute/wheels/ForceandInertia.php
Try some fun experiments with force, friction, gravity, and inertia at this site from the Illinois Math and Science Academy.

Little Shop of Physics
http://littleshop.physics.colostate.edu/amazingphysics.htm
At this website you will find experiments in force, energy, and motion, along with other basic physics concepts.

PBS Kids: Magnets and Gravity
http://pbskids.org/jayjay/care.curr.cl.l7.html
Videos and lessons on gravity—and an upside-down waterfall—can be found at this site.

Science Monster: Gravity and Inertia
http://www.sciencemonster.com/physical-science/gravity_inertia.html
Learning about gravity is fun and easy at this website, which features lessons and games about all branches of science.

Solar System Exploration
http://solarsystem.nasa.gov/kids/index.cfm
Find out your weight on different planets, build your own splace fleet, play planetary puzzles, and learn more fun facts about the solar system at this educational website from NASA.

StarChild: Black Holes
http://starchild.gsfc.nasa.gov/docs/StarChild/universe_level1/black_holes.html
Learn about black holes and how they form at this educational website from NASA.

INDEX

air, 14-15

black holes, 26-27

distance, 6, 12

Earth, 7
    falling objects on, 15
    formation of, 22
    inertia on, 16
    moon's orbit and, 20-21
    orbit of, 19
energy, 27

falling, 12-15
force, 5, 8-9
friction, 13-16

gravity, 4-7, 28-29
    black holes and, 26-27
    falling and, 12-13
    inertia and, 16
    in space, 10
    measuring, 8-9
    moon's, 10, 20-21
    sun's, 11, 18-19, 22-25

inertia, 16-19

Jupiter, 10, 16

mass, 5, 6, 20
    Earth's, 7
    measuring, 8
    moon's, 20
    weight *versus*, 10-11
matter, 6, 13
moon, 10, 15, 16, 20-21, 25
motion
    falling, 12-15
    inertia and, 16-17

Newton, Isaac, 17
newtons, 9

oceans, 21
orbits, 18-21

planets, 18-19, 22-25

solar system, 18-19, 22-25
space, 10, 16
speed. *See* motion
stars, 18, 26-27
sun, 11, 18-19, 22-25

tides, 21

universe, 4, 26, 28, 29

weight, 8-11